Cesarina Garcia Perth Amboy, NJ cesigpoetry.com
cesigpoetry@gmail.com

Book Layout, Cover and Design C2020 drylqd studio

Printed in the USA picked before bloom/Cesarina "cesi" Garcia
1st-Ed ISBN: 978-1-7360425-2-6

Thank You.

God, drylqd studio, eli, reggie, ma, pa, melina, mama paula, papa cesar, abuelita fin, master ricardo, corey, mario, janine, jess, justin, erinma, genesis, steph, darlz, keanu, mels and absolutely every single human i've ever crossed paths with in this plane. i love every single one of you.

This is a book about *cycles.* This is a book about *healing.* This is a book about *pain.* This is a book about inspiration, hesitation, self-esteem, self-doubt, self-hatred, self-sabotage, self-love, faith, desperation, reconciliation, judgment, gratitude and god. In its short duration, I hope you are able to read between the lines.

This book can be experienced two ways. You may read it and ignore this section entirely or you may choose to hover your phone camera over these QR codes and read along to the playlist I curated for Picked Before Bloom. Both are great.

i-TUNES   SPOTIFY

yesterday, my ride home was rerouted by a
truck who had hit a car.

most people see the big thing and assume
the big thing caused the incident.

"the truck hit the car" they reason; without
even knowing or being there.

but trucks are larger and carry a lot of mass,
at a slower velocity. they're hard to miss.

a small car can maneuver faster. it can dodge
and swerve with ease.

my life's been a lot like that scene.

a ricochet of blame between the big trucks and the
little cars.

and i'm the only driver.

there is no greater solitude than
acknowledging your own being.
nor a greater companionship.
who the fuck are you when there's no one around?

how blessed are we that we only occur for brief
happenings?
how beautiful it is to be an untold story.
never knowing how it ends.
how exciting it is to become –
a willingness that allows for peace.
for you, i wish an eternal internal inquisition.
so that you may find just how brightly you shine

the sun embraced me,

y me dejo ojos color a miel

luego, me beso mucho la piel.

sin miedo, sin desastre –

me ilumino la alma.

con deseo de amanecer.

if i told you literally
that my spirit met the moon,
under violet flames and bright white
lights
on an unbecoming root
you'd throw your head back with laugh-
ter
maybe slap a knee or two
but the ego tends to show
what it's like to be brand new
so until you reach me here,
i'll send lunar smiles to you.

in my dream we weren't drowning,
we were simply floating.
i could hear the earth's far cry
from the way the water coddled the ocean
imagine your source needed healing
like a sun needs recharging
picture if you will, your skin peeling
breaking from the essence of your being.
only needing faith to unravel.

maybe ants look at us,
the way we look at gods.
and blessings fall short,
because we pray too fast.
like giants in the sky,
begging for insignificance.

never realizing, truly, the greatness in
our presence.

in a universe of light, we stray
from incandescence

if the earth stood still to breathe you
in, don't let your soul desert you.

break to pieces on behalf of me
and let my memories mimic your history

be the past, the present and the
continuum theory.

14

who am i without the concrete? a sturdy, hard
lesson to learn. flowerless, mostly – usually begging to
grow.

who am i without the wind? a hard woman to love.
there's no fun in touching the ground.
i think i want to stay up here for a while.

who am i without the sun? a lifeless body grazes
the ocean floor.
without the kisses of the sunrise,
it's soul is begging to return.

who am i without the gentle autumn rain? a parched
mouth begins to decay.
Unearth words soon follow suit.
my mother told me to be silent or be cute.

who am i without god? i am the self without self.

i know someone who lives in perpetual hell.

he tried to reach the crown without the root.

        in the eyes of the becoming, my truth always fell short.

i hope you never rise up on someone else's name. because you'll fall by it too.

leaving you self less.

full of other.

unbeknownst to you.

there are days i forget your names
moments of fragmented freedom
where my memories are so oppressed
i temporarily don't taste disgust.

there's many things someone could steal

      but my childhood did not warrant robbery.
      it was cherished and enjoyed and revered.
      you do not realize how unsettling it feels
      to question your existence while you're still a kid.

      to conceptualize being.
      to look at the sky and want for more.

      i thank you.
      because of you, i've always wanted out
      i've wanted more than this skin.

i let my personhood fall
so i could step into spirithood
every day, i am aligned from within
every day, i am reborn.

why i gotta be the substance you lack?
who put you on this planet to retract?
do you even know that you're eternal?
did you know your existence is perpetual?
what kind of tongue tells lies?
is it made differently than mine?
who said somebody else makes you whole?
what kinda math figures so?
who taught you about being?
how come you never know what you're feeling?

the issue with eternity is that it's forever.

i kept falling in love with people hoping
i'd eventually fall in love with myself.

we were every season under the sun
except the right one
i know some day you'll find your solstice.
and this world won't know what to do with your light.

i had a dream i was a mother once
in blooms of sorrows i had beseeched.
the earth fell flat beneath my wings
and i was thereon marked by an equator of sin
i thought myself unworthy of the life i grew in
only stoic women can give birth to strong men
and i was perpetually written on wind.

i continue to long for the reality i perceived.
in this way, i know,
our winter will always give way to our spring.

my power is humbled by my humanity
i am the ever living queen of a lost mentality
my thoughts are obscured by a harsh reality
the ground i walk on is no place for mortality
and yet i continue to live.

to offend simply by breathing,
my lungs heap for fragilities.
if i were an angel, my wings would fail me –
let me tell you.
but only to remind me that love is a vulgarity and
that i do not belong on sacred ground.

despite my consistent cycles of repent, belief and sin
there are burning hot coals underneath my skin.

and i am the ever living blossom of a
mother with a heart too big.
incapable of learning to change –
i rise and i burn and i rise and i burn again.

   i am the phoenix of remiss –
   here to tell you that i've died and not yet lived.

be wary of the heart you claim a home
i am the human of a menace
and a troubled mind

i do not knock on doors,
i am simply inside.

and i do not break tables made

of glass –

i,

shatter with them.

i almost wrote a book about you.
this page was almost dedicated to you.
i almost told you i love you, still.
how i feel almost inexplicably linked to your being.

i almost text you to say i think of you.
how i think i can almost feel you still.
i think your memory is almost finally fading

i'm almost happy about that.

i want you to know i'm articulate
that i'm a bounty filled with the right words

i want you to understand my diction
how i don't walk, i stroll, with tongues

i am not pressed to be understood either
pressure only builds up until it bursts.

some see the shoes you just filled
and spend eternity trying to
figure out
who else can wear them.

i've learned lessons from bare feet.

your words left me alone with your presence
and i had no idea you were still becoming
i wish i knew what you were going to say before you
said it

i think in reverence, i prefer to hear your heart speak
i pray you know stillness by the time you finish

circles signify completion, or so i'm told
for you, i'll pray we return to the sun

on my best days i relished your toxicity
on my worst days, i became the smoke,
the lighter, and the tobacco

who knew pain would never leave your skin?
i know what it's like to live in your pores.
try not to imagine solace or salvation
it is never coming for the soul within you

if you're lucky, you'll only live a long and painful life
the rest of humanity will wash out before you
and you'll be stranded with your thoughts – at once.

and still,

i wish you peace.

if you died today,
could people mourn you in peace?

unencumbered by memories of your depth
how you touched the moon without her permission.
how you watered plants that were already drowning.
how you aspired despite transcendence.

god told me
not to overindulge
so i can only pass you by the wayside
and not look at you longingly;

like i really want to

dresses and the remaining caresses as
i dreamt of sore lines by the coat line.
your skin was made of tongues i kissed
and your hands,
a myriad of my favorite sins.

call out my name, like rain to raindrops

if pleasure exists without inhibitions,
then i am a harbor for love, never knowing gain.
your voice a thousand waves by the shore,
my heart a patient vessel for your phonics.

i met a snake charmer of a man once,
and i brought him directly to my grass.
i'm enthralled in the desert of his heart.

who knew love would be so dry?

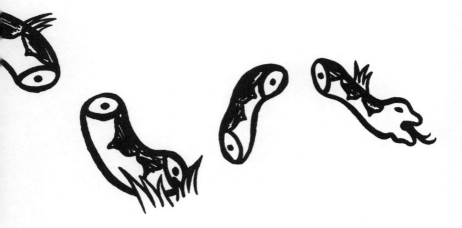

for a while, my soul told me to lay here
and play dead for your pleasantries.

if life's a bargain,
i hope you don't have buyer's remorse.

I lost myself in him,
but he asked me where I'd been.

how can you not tell i'm not
here anymore?

your words stay submerged in the sea of my feelings
steadily,
they flee.

what an audacious memory – to remember you.

you,

the soulless child with an indigo chest
lucky to have been born a purposeful mistake.

for a while, my poems about you had a hint of
shame
like a knife annoyed at a strong back –
indicative that it lacks self-awareness.

the child in me is still present.
hoping to regain the remnants of what she lost in
your essence
not knowing if at all any of it had been her fault
unquestionably demanding –

are these really the fucking cards i've been dealt?

en la península que olvidablemente se dibuja
como una isla
en las mañanas de plátano maduro con huevos her-
vidos
donde tres golpes es comida, y no una frase violenta
en los cacaos de san francisco de macorís, ahí me crie
yo.

donde la ignorancia y religión niega
lo que pasa adentro de los hogares comunes
donde la culpa queda adentro del cuerpo de un niño
violado
llegan a preguntar qué porque a cambiado y al final,
es el silencio que lo ha matado.

ahí en mi campo,
donde mire hacia al cielo, queriendo hablar con dios
para gritarle, llorarle y rogarle, "¿porque yo?"
solo encontré estrellas que me decían

"que hermoso es existir."

who knew that the coarseness of our
labored hymns would one day make
our voices strong?

picked before bloom:
flowers picked too soon.

from stems expected to flourish,
men found themselves malnourished.

bearing prickled, blood-stained palms,
our forced blossoms turned to bombs.

exploding on unforgiving souls,
praying that prayers made us whole.

Cesarina "Cesi" Garcia

Cesarina "Cesi" Garcia is a Dominican immigrant residing in New Jersey. She's a lover of life, viewing everything as poetry – she aspires to help other humans overcome their trauma by changing how they view it. This book is simply the start of her artistic expression and earnest contribution to everyone existing on Earth.

She may be reached at cesigpoetry.com, via email at cesigpoetry@gmail.com or on Twitter and Instagram @cesigpoetry.

If you or anyone you know needs assistance or wishes to speak to someone about sexual abuse, molestation or harassment, please check out these resources:

RAINN (Rape, Abuse & Incest National Network):
+1. 800.656.4673

NSVRC (National Sexual Violence Resource Center):
https://www.nsvrc.org/find-help

Lightning Source UK Ltd.
Milton Keynes UK
UKHW051046040122
396383UK00003B/30